SIDNEY PICKLES

Adventures on Jeju Island, South Korea

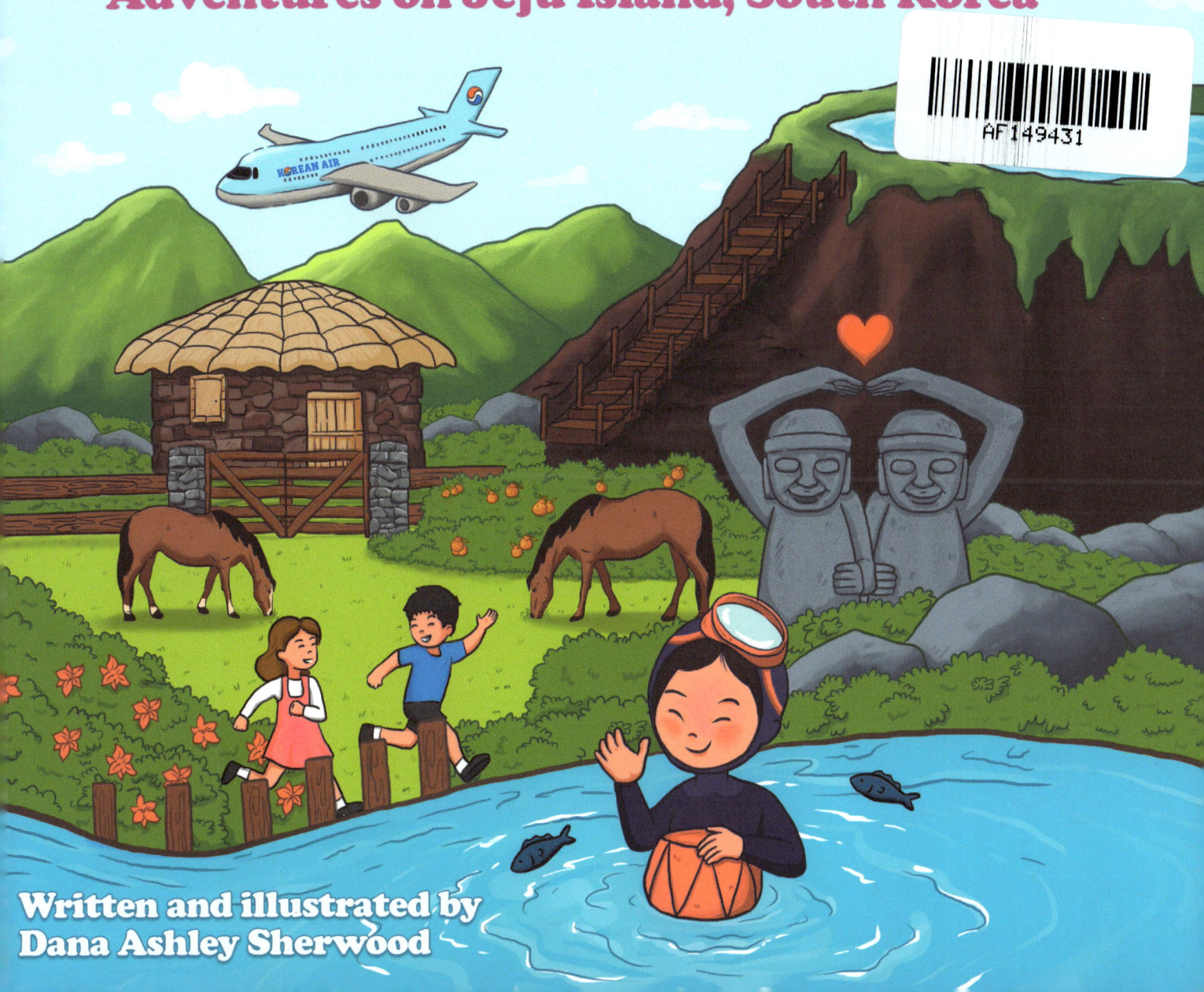

Written and illustrated by
Dana Ashley Sherwood

BookSide Press
877-741-8091
www.booksidepress.com
orders@booksidepress.com

DEDICATION

Dedicated to my Bear Bear and Little Peanut. The island of our beginning, where we floated on our dreams, sailed through waves, wondered, and wished about the future.

Today is an adventure, and I'm ready for my flight! Off to Jeju Island to see some amazing sights. My magnifying glass is in my hand, and I'm ready to explore; Jeju and it's coastal shores.

Jeju Island was formed from volcanic activity, and lies in the Korea Strait. As I am driving along the coast, I see nature all around and hear many different sounds.

Hallasan Mountain is my first stop! It is the highest mountain in the Korea Strait and has a lot of steps that are steep to climb. The view from the top is divine!

Cheonjiyeon Waterfall is next on my list. I hope I get a little wet from its mist. Into my wetsuit just in case, but no swimming allowed, it's not safe!

There are stone statues known as Dol harubang (stone grandfather) everywhere I look. Friendly faces have an aged look. The guardians of Jeju are strong and true. They are easy to find because they are always looking at you!

It's time to eat; so much to choose from! Traditional delights, here I come!

In South Korea, some staple foods are meat, vegetables, and rice. Don't forget to add a little kimchi and spice!

My favorite discovery is a mural you see! It is a Haenyeo (female diver), a woman of the sea. Haenyeo harvest mollusks, seaweed, and fish, to make a delicious dish.

Haenyeo are famous on this island. They are part of its foundation and history. Amazing women who free dive (breath-holding dive), in the ocean so deep. Haenyeo can float without treading water, like fish in the sea!

Olle Trails cover the island: hiking, walking, and biking are in style. Everywhere you look, you can see hills, green trees, and blue ocean for miles.

Jeju has volcanic ash-rich soil, as you can see, with many flowers and fields aplenty.

Up next on my trip is Bijarim Forest. I walk along a winding trail and smell the nutmeg trees. A forest from the past, with a history that has continued to last.

Time to sail on the deep blue sea and snorkel on the surface. What will I see? From the boat, I look towards the coast and see two Pony lighthouses. What a sight, one is red and the other is white!

After snorkeling, I travel to Jeju-si, an island city with variety. The roundabouts are a wild show, car and truck drivers know when to go.

As the green pedestrian light blinks go, I walk across the street and raise my hand because that's a signal all drivers understand.

When I'm hungry, I stop for a treat at food trucks that are glamorous and unique.

Traditional treats are along the streets. Tteok (simmered rice cakes), coffles (croissant waffles), taiyaki (fish-shaped pastry), and bingsu (shaved ice dessert) to name a few, are sweet and delicious, too.

YAKGWA

TTEOK

PAIBINGSOO

CROFFLES

TAIYAKI

BINGSU

Jeju Island lies in the Korea Strait. It is a natural wonder; a safe and fun place!

Going home on the airplane, I think about sharing my adventures with friends. Maybe someday I will visit Jeju Island again.

Sidney Pickles signing out!
- 감사합니다 gamsahabnida (Thank you)

www.ingramcontent.com/pod-product-compliance
Lightning Source LLC
Chambersburg PA
CBHW042201060526
44654CB00035B/453